A Year in Woolacombe & Morte

AND OTHER RAMBLINGS OF A SERIOUSLY-DISTURBED MAN

BY STEVE BROWN
(AUTHOR OF 'ON MY HOME GROUND')

Moonwolf Books

If you don't need to know it – 'tis probably in yer

FOREWORD BY SHARON REES

Those who read, and enjoyed, Steve's first book, **'On My Home Ground'**, as I did, will be delighted with this sequel where, once again, we are immersed in the life of our two villages.

Written with warmth and humour, the reader is introduced to more village 'characters' – some real, some the figment of his vivid imagination; all coupled with anecdotes and quotes of a spiritual nature.

As one reviewer put it '. . . *a lost world but still in our hearts'*. I thoroughly recommend this little book.

AUTHOR'S NOTE

It has been a great privilege to write for the local newspapers and magazines over the past years and I hope that old and new readers will enjoy this book. I am indebted to many people for their encouragement, in particular Sue Hill for her tireless encouragement, editing and advice, to Nathan Payne, Caroline Dyck, Rona Watson, Gwyneth Bennelick, Nikki Payne, Shirley Bowden, Sharon Rees and John Phillips, and also to everyone for the kind comments on *'On My Home Ground'*.

The jottings are my own, apart from where stated, but the 'Thoughts of the Month' have been ruthlessly plagiarised from writers far more eloquent and witty than I.

I have been persuaded by Sue to include the 'dialect pieces'. I am ever conscious of Oscar Wilde's remark that *'It is impossible for an Englishman with an accent to open his mouth without another Englishman taking an instant dislike to him'* and it is apparent to me that what might seem whimsical, and mildly enjoyable, to some, will surely grate on the ears of others (and may even be incomprehensible). My apologies in advance.

Published in May 2016 by Moonwolf Books, Arden, Sunnyside Road, Woolacombe, North Devon, EX34 7DG. Email: stephenbrown1949@aol.com Tel: 01271 870538

ISBN: 978-1-5262032-0-5
All text copyright Steve Brown
Colour photographs copyright Atmosphere Publishing Ltd. and The Picture Postcard Company UK; all available from outlets in the two villages.
Printed by Toptown Printers Ltd., Vicarage Lawn, Barnstaple, N. Devon EX32 7BN

Accolades for Steve Brown's first book:
'On My Home Ground'
(available from stephenbrown1949@aol.com)

Loved the book. You really got the atmosphere of the times right. D.G.

I actually laughed 'til I cried. P.H.

It's brilliant, I *really* enjoyed it from start to finish. T.M.

It took me back to my school days – thoroughly enjoyed every page. D.Y.

Am loving the book, it's just brilliant. What a treasure – a lost world but still in our hearts. Howls of laughter to the description of the 60s' clothes. G.L.

Thoroughly enjoyed it. G.Y.

Many thanks for the laughter and nostalgia you have given me on reading your wonderful book. A little gem and greatly enjoyed – looking forward to the sequel. S.J.

Have just had a visit from a local lad who said he laughed all the way through it. The humour generated was an excellent aid to digestion after Christmas excesses. J.P.

Charming. (S.B. has) a delightful writing style and I cannot wait for the sequel. J.K.

Witty and very amusing. R.E.

Brilliant, I loved every page. T.S.

Read with much enjoyment and a lot of laughter. What a joy this book is. K.H.

Wonderful. Thoroughly enjoyed it. M.R.

Kept my brother amused. I could hear him laughing out loud all evening. V.L.

I laughed till I cried..............had me in stitches. E.B.

Laughter and Nostalgia. F.B.

What can I say? Your book is a little bijou which has entertained me, out loud even, for the past two days. It's not that I'm a slow reader but I wanted to savour it uninterrupted. Thank you for the reminiscing and the laughter you brought - I'm always very grateful for any joy in my life. You do have a gift for writing so when will the next one be out? C.D.

A fantastic, funny read. Well done. S.P.

JANUARY

THOUGHTS ON THE NEW YEAR

I commence in a mood of optimism.

For those, like myself, who struggle with the dark days and long nights of winter, let us take comfort in the thought that we have passed the shortest day, and Spring will soon be with us. This we can enjoy in beauty and simplicity and I make no apologies for repeating what, to me, are the most inspiring and enchanting words:

'Gradually from destruction will come new life.

After the storms and the winds have blown through the world there always comes the new life of Spring. When the winds blow and all looks bleak, you are not able to see the freshness of Spring, but it comes.

And gradually, as the great sun of life moves through the heavens, so the majesty of life comes to its fullest. Then will come the Spring of Dreams and the Summer of Fulfilment.'

—ooOoo—

Now I turn to another wonder – that of medicine and, in particular, the advancements in understanding the human psyche. Yet a nagging thought occurs.

Let me take you back to Woolacombe Primary School – the date is the mid 1950s, the beginning of term and the new arrivals:

'Mr Rigby, you'll have to be very careful with young Tyrone. He has XYZ symptom.'

'XYZ Symptom, Mrs Stoatweasel? XYZ SYMPTOM! I'll give him XYZ symptom. I think you'll find when I've banged his head against the blackboard enough times he'll soon forget about his XYZ symptom.'

'Well, yes, Mr Rigby, I'm sure you know best but…..'

'Yes, Mrs Stoatweasel, I think you'll find that I do know best.'

'Well, alright Mr Rigby, I must leave it up to you.'

I make no comment.

—ooOoo—

With my customary *Grumpy Old Man's* hat on, I turn to yet another of we oldies' mainstays in life which seems to be disappearing and I refer to the jolly old Telephone Directory.

How 'thin' this publication has become. Why, even I, as a grown-up *seven-stone weakling*, could probably manage to tear one of these in half. (Younger readers please ask your grandparents for an explanation of that last statement.) But this is a serious matter.

For decades, when we needed to contact anyone who was not an intimate, we 'looked them up in the Directory', as everyone was listed for all to see and contact. That was how things were done – properly - and it worked. But now, since the advent of the 'nuisance' sales calls, virtually everyone is *'ex-directory'*, a status once reserved for 'important' people (or those who thought of themselves as such).

I used to be fond of telling people how they could save money – 'No need to buy an address book,' said I, 'just keep the old Telephone Directory and cross out all the people you don't know.' Unfortunately, no-one understands this anymore.

So when I was ensconced in the Lamb Inn, Ilfracombe and needed a phone I asked the barmaid if I could avail myself and, for the princely sum of £1, yes one pound, she allowed me to do so. But, when I asked to 'borrow the directory,' which I thought to be a perfectly reasonable request, she was astounded. It was as if I had asked her *(Publisher's Note - delete next few words.)*

So, I am told by my young work colleagues that this is all 'old hat'. We now look the number up on the internet. Now, I am not a Luddite – I haven't smashed up a loom for, well, at least five years - but I have to tell you that this simply doesn't work.

I was recently accused by a fellow campaigner of being 'ex-directory'. 'I don't trust people who are ex-directory,' she told me.

'But I am not – check page 182 – third column, 2" down.'

'Oh,' came the reply, 'I didn't check in the book, I looked you up on the internet and you weren't listed.'

Now, forgive me, but I am not ex-directory. Whether I am *ex-internet*, if such a thing exists, I couldn't say, but this clearly proves the ineffectiveness of said system. If people who are still in the directory (that word again) cannot be found on the internet then what is the point?

No doubt someone under the age of seven will be able to explain the benefits of the modern method but, for me, could we not (a) ban all nuisance calls – with heavy penalties for transgressing this law and (b) all go back into the Telephone Directory, please? Then it really would be something to boast that you could tear it in two.

OVERHEARD OUTSIDE THE PUFFIN CAFÉ:

"Well my buay, eev dun very well fer ees self and eev bought a' house in the poshest rawd in Woolacombe."

"Git on with ee, Maid."

"No, Mildred, tis true. He reckons some of ee's nairbours reads the Daily Telegraph, and plays golf."

"Not at the saime taame?"

"No, course not at the saime taaime, yer maize fule. Anyway, ees got nairbours 'oo drave Volvos, and one of em wears a trilby 'at."

" What the Volvo?"

"Now you'm just being silly cos you'm jealous."

"Naw ahm not - anyway, that's naught, Maivis. Where mah daughter lives in the parish, one of the 'ouses down the rawd 'ev just been bought as a second 'ome by a laidy from London who talks in a silly affected voice, and calls 'er mother 'Mummy'. Now tell me, yu can't get posher than that can 'ee?"

Long Silence. "Ow's yer husband anyway?"

INTERESTING FACT NUMBER ONE (or not as you decide)

I encountered a holidaymaker taking great interest in the post box at the bottom of Rockfield Road which is an 'Edward VII' and thus, apparently, very rare. To be honest, I had never really taken any notice of the monarch's name on our post boxes but they are clearly designated and, due to the antiquity and relative shortness of said King's reign, these particular ones are in very short supply.

No doubt our esteemed Planning and Conservation Officers will welcome plans to turn it into a mobile phone booth or similar.

Yes, I know, I should get out more.

THOUGHTS FOR THE MONTH

What are we without the beasts? If all the beasts were gone we would die from great loneliness of spirit, for whatever happens to the beasts also happens to us. All things are connected. Whatever befalls the earth befalls the children of the earth. (Anonymous American Indian.)

I don't know how to save the world. I don't have the answers or The Answer. I only know that, without compassion and respect for all of Earth's inhabitants, none of us will survive – nor will we deserve to. (Leonard Peltier).

FEBRUARY

Well, thank goodness January is now passed and we have completed the nadir of our *winter of discontent.*

In one particularly bleak week, of the ten hostelries in the parish, no less than seven were closed. It's enough to drive a man to drink (if he could find anywhere open).

I well remember remarking to a fellow parishioner how Woolacombe was still very much a 'one horse town' and being told, *'Yes, and if you come here in January you can be forgiven for thinking that somebody has stolen the b***** horse!'* Some things never change.

—ooOoo—

I relate a lovely account from the Ward-Locke guide which, as an amateur wordsmith, gives me great pleasure to read:

"Woolacombe: Where the sands are long and golden and pools of sea water are mirrors of the sky's perfect blue, where there are miniature ravines and carpets of heather ablaze on the moors, close-clipped grass for the tired limb, fields of corn crowning the summit of the hills and, at one's feet, a million dancing, waves."

How delightful to see the English language used in such an evocative way!

OLD WOOLACOMBE & MORTE CHARACTERS 1

I quote the true tale of a lady who worked in the stillroom at the Woolacombe Bay. It was an August day in the 1960s and I was leaving my morning shift in the 'wash up' when I encountered her in South Street accosting a 'Bay' guest and, as many will tell you, the more affluent visitors of the day reflected their status in their general bearing and dress code. This gentleman, and he was a gentleman, was suitably attired in a linen suit and Panama hat, and one could easily imagine him to be a consultant surgeon or similar as he listened to the following diatribe:

"Wull, what us looks vorward to at this taame of year is next month when us gets a much better class of visitor down yer. What us ev got now – us won't say tis riffraff exacley - us won't zay that - but tis not the type of person us laakes to zee in Woolacombe and tis much more classy next month. That's what us laakes."

I wondered what said gentleman was thinking as he nodded pensively, clearly appreciating the fact that Marion (for it was she) didn't consider him to be 'exactly riffraff'.

'A NIGHT TO REMEMBER'

It is now more than one hundred years since the loss of the Titanic yet, for me, the fascination of the great liner, and the final tragedy, is as addictive as ever – the alleged prophesies of disaster, the premonitions, the extraordinary destiny of those who were on board by chance, and those who fortuitously missed the sailing; the sheer opulence of the first-class accommodation; even the inventory of items that went to the bottom of the sea remains morbidly seductive, but I fully understand others who feel that enough is enough and those who lost their lives should be allowed to rest in peace.

Nonetheless, a rather interesting analogy crosses my mind as I study the endless tales of the doom-laden voyage.

It is well-documented that your chance of survival on that fateful night rested mainly on the price of your ticket. First-class passengers' lives were clearly of the utmost importance, second-class to a definite lesser degree, and steerage, well, steerage passengers could not expect too much assistance, particularly if their rescue in any way hampered the saving of their 'betters'.

Walter Lord's excellent book *'A Night to Remember'* is still arguably the seminal account, and the basis for the epic film of the same name. In an interesting digression, he gives some fascinating insights into Edwardian wealth and social status and I quote:

'The night was a magnificent confirmation of 'women & children first' and yet somehow the loss was greater for third-class children than first-class men.'

The subsequent enquiry looked into every conceivable avenue, including, bizarrely, what an iceberg was made of (*'Ice'* explained Fifth Officer Lowe), and yet only three third-class passengers were called as witnesses, two of whom stated that they were 'prevented from accessing the lifeboats'. This was never followed up – not because of any alleged cover-up, merely that nobody seemed to be that interested.

It is a sad reflection on the materialism and class-consciousness of the day and Walter Lord states *'… the Titanic was the last stand of wealth and society in the centre of public affection.'*

Replace the word 'society' with 'celebrity' and Mr Lord's words have a hollow ring in twenty-first century Britain.

I quote from Mr Lord again:

'The preoccupation was fully appreciated by the press. When the Titanic sank, the 'New York Times' listed the prominent passengers on the front page. The 'New York American'

broke the news with a leader devoted entirely to John Jacob Astor and at the end it mentioned that '…. 1,800 others were also lost….'.'

In similar mood, the 18th April *'New York Sun'* covered the insurance angle of the disaster. Most of the story concerned Mrs Widener's pearls.

Why do I mention all of this now? It is simply that I see a return to this vulgar fixation on wealth and social status after the intervening century.

Fast forward almost one hundred years and an executive of MacLaren, speaking on the marketing policy for their new supercar (priced at £675,000 some ten years ago) opined:

*'We were purposely limiting the number produced to one hundred. We knew that we could easily sell that number of cars (at close to ¾ million pounds) throughout the world, and we had to bear in mind that **all of the buyers would almost certainly know each other.'***

One hundred people of totally different nationalities, languages, occupations, religions etc., scattered throughout the world – the only common denominator being excessive wealth - *and they would all know each other*?

Why should this be and does it not strike you as extraordinary and slightly unnerving? Is there not a parallel when Walter Lord wrote of the *Titanic* first class passengers:

'….those who enjoyed this kind of life gradually became part of a remarkably tight little group.

… There was a wonderful intimacy about this little world of Edwardian rich. There was not a flicker of surprise when they bumped into each other at the Pyramids (a great favourite), Cowes Regatta or the springs at Baden Baden. So the Titanic's trip was more like a reunion than an ocean passage.'

Although it is true that 'poverty' has a different interpretation to that endured by our Edwardian forefathers, the colossal disparity between the reported earnings of bankers and others in the media, sport and industry etc. and the remuneration of the ordinary (hard-) working man and woman seems once again to be accelerating. (This is to say nothing of the millions in other parts of our planet who are dying for want of nothing more than basic nourishment or clean drinking water.)

Perhaps the landed gentry no longer represent the glamour in our ever-more valueless society but we now have footballers (and their 'wives'), 'reality' T.V. stars and talent show contestants to assume the mantle.

If, God forbid, the twenty-first century *Titanic* disaster occurred, who would bet against much of today's popular press leading with the 'glamour' of the rich and famous who had been lost, and the cost of their accoutrements, before the footnote that *'1,800 other 'ordinary' souls had also perished'* ?

To quote Pete Seeger: *'When will they ever learn?'*

—ooOoo—

OVERHEARD IN THE VILLAGE HALL:

"Yer, 'ev 'ee yerd about they shenanigins up at the Church, Maivis?"

"No, what 'appened?"

"Wull, they wanted zome outzide paintin' done zo they got quotes from two local traidesmen – gude quotes they wus too. Anyway, along comes this chap and zaid he'd do it cheaper. Wull, they dezided to use 'un, BUT, a week after 'eed vinished the job, it started rairnin' and all the paint washed off – twas rinnin' down the rawd."

"Get on with 'ee."

"Wull, they called 'n back and 'ee admitted 'eed thinned down all the pairnts so's 'ee could cut the price. Ainyway, 'ee wuz very,very zorry. Apparently, 'ee kneeled down in the church aisle in for vront of the Vicar and vowed ee'd *repaint and thin no more.*"

Sorry, not very original I know but this is a local book – you're not going to get Oscar Wilde.

THOUGHTS FOR THE MONTH

The problem with the world is that the intelligent people are full of doubts, while the stupid ones are full of confidence. (Charles Bukowski).

We are put on this earth to help others. What the others are put here for has yet to be satisfactorily explained.

MARCH

THOUGHTS ON THE IMMINENT ARRIVAL OF SPRING

Is it not extraordinary that, as I write this, the warm sun is blazing down whilst the news headlines advise of severe snow in the Northern part of the country? Once again, we seem to have avoided nature's extremes here in the Westcountry.

At the moment we can delight in the profusion of daffodils, celandines, primroses and buttercups around our parish and I often wonder whether it is coincidental that the early spring flowers all seem to be yellow?

Isn't it GREAT to see the sun? And what a fantastic start to the season!

Longer days lead me into the Garden Centres, and it brings such pleasure to see the feast of bedding plants on display. What a fabulous time of year.

As you will have guessed, your humble scribe is feeling the *joys of spring,* but my foray into the possible purchase of some garden furniture soon brought me back to reality. How nice it looks. Could I afford it? But wait, note the three little words that we non– do-it-yourselfers dread – *Easy Self-Assembly.*

Now, speaking as one who thought *'two b' one'* was an African dictator, I contend that the words 'easy' and 'self-assembly' should *never* appear in the same sentence. Many years ago I was told that 'Sex is like MFI furniture – very few get it together the first time', but why is it that some people manage to accomplish things with such ease, whereas the rest of us labour in an orgy of anger, frustration and, ultimately, disappointment? And what exactly is the pleasure in DIY?

I rather like the advice given by a fellow D.I.Y. failure: *'The only two items you really need in a tool box are WD40 and Duct Tape (or is that Duck Tape – I'm never sure?).'* Anyway, the theory goes that, if it moves and it shouldn't, then you need Duct Tape and, if it doesn't move and it should, then use WD40.

Brilliant but simple.

Thinking again of spring and the frog spawn which is now starting to develop, I am fond of this quotation from an unnamed source:

'I have always liked frogs. I like the look of frogs, I like their outlook – especially the way they get together in wet places on warm evenings to sing about procreation.

If we can discover the meaning of the trilling of a frog perhaps we may understand why, for us, it is not merely a noise but a song of poetry and emotion.'

—ooOoo—

It is interesting to note the reappearance of the long, narrow 'lake' at the far end of the Warren, a feature which I had quite forgotten until recently reminded by several local 'boys' (all now well over the age of sixty).

When we were young, in the 1950s, there was always a small lake, which might have partially dried out in a particularly hot summer but was nonetheless a constant. At some stage this disappeared, only to return a few years ago.

In addition, the top part of the beach immediately below now continues to lie wet long after the tide has receded. Are the two facts connected, and is this due to the excessive rainfall last year, thus suggesting that there had been insufficient to create this phenomenon for the intervening fifty plus years?

I will leave it to someone with more detailed knowledge of such matters.......

A FURTHER ARTICLE ON THE PARISH this time from a later Warde-Locke guide:

'It is not surprising that with such wealth of beauty, Woolacombe is a seaside resort of rapidly growing importance. A very few years ago it consisted of a farm and some labourers' cottages. Now it has hotels and boarding houses, attractive private residences, banks and row of shops. The site has been judiciously laid out, and building regulations prevent erections which would degrade the character of the place. It is necessary to write some time ahead for accommodation both at Woolacombe and Mortehoe, which are now separated only by a short distance of cliff road.

Woolacombe has grown up at the end of the usual Devon combe, which, however, is much more open and less wooded than some, giving a consequent impression of freedom. On the east, olive-tinted, white-fringed rocks lie like monsters out to sea, separated by lovely sandy coves. Here and there are gleaming white quartz veins in the grey cliffs, gloriously crowned with grass and yellow sea flowers.

At the northern part of the bay, backed by Mortehoe, olive-tinted, white-fringed rocks pointing finger-like to sea are separated by lovely sandy coves.'

OLD WOOLACOMBE & MORTEHOE CHARACTERS 2

My first employer, and mentor, the village grocer:

"Kris'fer, (I was always Christopher for reasons I know not but you get used to it) Kris'fer, I was on the bus comin' back vrum 'Combe and the bliddy laidy next ter me – er couldn't vind 'er purse, er wus viddling about saw much I zaid, 'I'll pay yer vare me dear'."

"Oh," er zaid, "that's very kind of 'ee but why would you want ter do that?"

"Well," I zaid, "You've undone me fly button dree tames whaale you bin messing about traaying ter vand yer purse."

It was a delight to observe the dear man dealing with the lady customers. A simple request such as

"Mr Miles, can I have half a pound of ham?" would be answered by:

"My booty, you ken 'ev the shirt off my back if you want, you naw that dawnt 'ee? Baay the way, you'm looking bootiful ma dear."

'Every little' may *'help'* but you don't get treated like that at Tesco.

—ooOoo—

I recently read a copy of my favourite newspaper and, turning to the 'Travel' section, an article on Venice caught my eye. Those of us - and I guess I am talking about 90% of the readership – who were keen to see a photograph of the subject were to be disappointed, or partially so.

The left side of the city is in clear view but the right is deliberately obscured by a huge picture of George Clooney with a woman whom we are told is Sandra Bullock. The reason for their inclusion? Apparently, they once attended a film festival there – a tenuous link, surely, in anyone's view.

Now I am sure that those who wish to view pictures of said Sandra Bullock can find plenty to satisfy them on the internet. But this is supposed to be an article about *Venice*.

Notwithstanding, we commence to read and are told immediately, for reasons that are not made clear, that the writer has a baby with the unfortunate name of 'Zephyr'. (Well, after the pretentious drivel in the opening paragraph it is unlikely she would have a *Mary* or an *Ann.*)

Armed with this nugget, the reader ploughs on, but we end up better informed about her family, and said George Clooney and Sandra Bullock, than the city in question.

Is this how it is done today? Perhaps I am out of step, but suffice to say, I found it rather disappointing. However, I have resisted the temptation to describe it as a *load of Bullocks.* (Neither will I obscure part of my text with pictures of celebrities or rabbit on about my children, *Tarquin* and *Jocasta* – delightful as they, of course, are.)

THOUGHTS FOR THE MONTH

It is receiving that gives us a living, but giving that gives us a life.

An expert is a man who can tell you tomorrow why what he forecast yesterday didn't happen today.

APRIL

PARADE HOUSE (AGAIN!)

St Paul's Letter to the Combemartians Chapter 1

And, lo, there was at that time a magnificent palace in the land known as Woolacombe, which in Hebrew means *Place of the expensive beer*, and peoples came from many miles.

But, in the year of our Lord 2014 a wandering infidel came upon the place and shouted, 'I will smite this building as the locust smiteth the dung beetle. I will leave the people of Woolacombe with an unholy structure which shall forever be likened to a public bathhouse and it will give me riches liken unto King Soloman.'

But the good peoples of the land rose up as one in their anger and there was much lamenting and gnashing of (false) teeth.

And it came to pass there was amongst them an holy man who spent his days in silent contemplation, studying ancient scripts and reading the Daily Telegraph, and he cried aloud, 'I will stand up and fight this monster with my mighty *Section 134 Legislation (Para 64 verse 4) of Righteousness,* and he donned a sackcloth garb and said, 'I will not remove this until the infidel is banished and his plans brought to dust' (well, not literally, but thou gettest my meaning).

But the elders and scribes in the land known as *Barn-staple*, which is to say 'Place of the arrogant ones', were the rulers over the lands of Woolacombe. And they, led by Mary of Pool and others who worshipped at the Hall of Collette, were sore annoyed with the peoples of the land and vowed to rebuke them as the seagull doth rebuke over the sunworshippers upon the beach.

But there was, in their number, a good and holy man (there were a lot of holy men) known as St. Malcolm of Wilkinson, who dwelt in the land of *Bankterrace* which is to say in Hebrew *'Road leading to Cowlers Garage'*. And, lo, St Malcolm fell foul of his brethren and cried aloud, 'I will not stand with the other elders and scribes. And I will write an epistle which will bring terror to their hearts and, lo, even the very vaults of the Civic Temple shall tremble at my words.'

But the elders poured scorn on St Malcolm as the camel poureth (well, thou gettest the picture).

And the peoples waxed sore annoyed. But there was at that time, dwelling in the place that is Leicestershire, which is to say in Hebrew *Place of the Premiership Football Champions,* a holy man (yes, another holy man) and he cried out in anguish, 'They shall not desecrate this holy site and I have an barrister who will put a stop to it.'

And thus it came to pass that the elders and scribes were made to eat their words as the camel eateth the dung in the Desert that is Gobi.

And at that time there lived in the land of *Arden* a hermit by the name of Brother Stephen, a simple man who was unable to contemplate anything other than how to slake his mighty thirst. And it came to pass one evening, after Br. Stephen had imbibed at the Well of the Smugglers Rest (only £3.00 per pint in the winter months) that the Brother received an vision (or he believeth that it was an vision) and Lo, an Angel said, 'Thou art a simple man but thou shalt lead an army of six or even seven brave souls who will also rise up against the Arrogant Ones.' And Brother Stephen was sore pleased so he went back in and imbibed some more.

But the unholy one prayed to the higher God, he that dwelleth in the place named *Bristol,* and the Mighty Inspector looked upon the infidel and cried, 'Indeed thou hath been sorely treated by the peoples of that place and, in my wrath, I shall inflict upon them thy hideous temple. Go forward then and take thine Outline Planning Consent as a sign that I am the Omnipotent One and thou shalt have no other Planning Inspector other than me.'

Then the unholy one cried, 'I have had enough of the peoples of this land. They do not worship my temple and they clearly do not appreciate the greatness of my advisors.' And thus he removed himself from the land, taking only three hundred thousand shekels profit to comfort him in his sorrow and disappointment. And the multitude sat in dread of the forthcoming defilement that was to be put amongst them.

Here endeth the first lesson.

—ooOoo—

First complaint of the holiday season and Mrs Flangebucket cannot get the television to work.

"Well," zaid I, "'tis simple."

"Us'll get Mr Adams out vrom Combe Martin to check th' aerial (that's th' 'H' shairped thing on the top of the roof. You must have seed they everywhere." (Come to think of it, I ebn seed many laitely – but no matter.)

"Then ee'll eve a look at the zet – check 'tis all in working order and switch on. If you wait vive minutes for 'n to warm up yoo shude get a perfect little black & white picture. If I mind c'rrectly, setting number 2 is BBC and number 7 is ITV, if you ken get it."

"Oh, and if Jack Smith is using ees 'lectric drill, you warn zee nought apart from a load of squiggly lines zo you'll eve ter wait till ees vanished."

What d'ee think? Er zaid her was packing her bags and gwain ter zomewhere more modern. Visiters t'day – you can't mek 'em out can ee?

ON BECOMING AN OLD AGE PENSIONER

May I just thank everyone for their congratulations and well wishes on your humble scribe finally becoming a fully-fledged old age pensioner? I have purchased the flat cap and am being measured for the official old men's trousers i.e. those that sit just below chest height. I shall then be in possession of the answer to that mystery that befuddles all young people: Exactly how do those trousers stay up?

It is a well-accepted fact that, the older men become, the higher their trousers are and I read somewhere of a man in Russia who attained the age of 112. Presumably his trousers finish just below his eyes, but there is a serious issue here which I would like to share with you.

I have long pondered the increasing old-age population. Many young people born today will achieve their century and it is suggested that subsequent generations will surpass that. Is this sustainable? Will average lifespans continue to increase? I think not, and the reason lies in the simple trouser.

Mother Nature is a clever old bird and has latched on to this philosophy. Clearly, at the present ratio of age to trouser-height, men will not be very far into their 120s before the trouser waistband reaches, and covers, the eyes. (One has to presume that a new form of braces that hook over the ears will be the norm by then.)

But there you have it. Old men will be wandering around, their eyes covered by their trousers, bumping into things and each other, causing themselves serious injury and death. Thus it is not, in my humble opinion, possible for men to live beyond 130 at the most, and the whole thing will be self-limiting due to our old friend, the trouser.

OLD WOOLACOMBE & MORTEHOE CHARACTERS 3

I'm going to change the name of the next one, although most will recognise him. I relate to the great days of the Fortescue with dear Peter Shelley behind the bar and an early evening regular was something of a hero of mine. Described as 'the best car salesman in North Devon' and I have absolutely no idea on what that was based, he was, none the less, a glamourous figure to me and, as my father would have said, "If a person can maintain their *upper-class accent* when they are totally drunk it is probably genuine."

As a naïve nineteen-year-old, I used to hang around in the hope that words of wisdom would eschew from his lips and one day I was not to be disappointed. "Stevie", said he throwing his arm around my neck, "Stevie, what are you doing now?"

Excitedly I responded, "Well, *Bill,* I am selling long-life light bulbs door to door."

"Stevie," said he, his grip ever-tightening, "Stevie, always remember that selling long-life lightbulbs is like making love to a beautiful woman."

And I always remembered it. What it means, I haven't a clue but remember it I certainly did.

THE CAFÉ SOCIETY

Having, no doubt, bored you rigid with my views on our parish, I turn my attention to Ilfracombe and a headline in the 'Journal': *Pedestrian plan branded idiotic and confusing* and, whereas I have no comment to make on the proposal, I am intrigued to hear once again reference to that fascinating subject, the 'Café Culture'.

Now far be it from me to dampen anyone's enthusiasm regarding Ilfracombe High Street, with which I have a long and, largely, happy association. Looking at our beloved main thoroughfare at the present time, it is true that the image of Parisian-style *fashionistas* gaily sipping lattes and glasses of Merlot is, indeed, enticing; however, I have to wonder, albeit reluctantly, whether we may be setting our sights a little high?

I am also curious as to just how many catering establishments are required to formulate a 'café culture' and, more presciently, could they all make a living?

I have fond memories of the early 1970s and 'Terry's Café' at number 88 when it was often necessary to pay for the *Sausage Egg & Chips Special* in advance in order that the proprietor could pop over to Ford & Lock's to purchase the sausages because 'things were a bit tight' and I have a sneaking feeling that 'things' are still pretty taut today.

Over the past forty years we have witnessed many hard-working, enterprising individuals open cafés and restaurants in the High Street. Not many have stayed the course and I am left with the inescapable conclusion that it was lack of business, rather than any other factor, that brought about their downfall.

Perhaps I have misunderstood the situation, but I feel that it would be particularly interesting to hear the views of past and present café-owners on the sustainability of said 'café culture' before we become once again lost in unachievable dreams over the revitalisation of our town.

My solution? There are simply far too many shops for our twenty-first century car-driving, Tesco-supporting, internet-shopping populace. Allow conversion of empty and redundant retail units into quality housing and give our remaining shopkeepers a chance.

THOUGHTS FOR THE MONTH

Eleanor Roosevelt was delighted to have a rose named after her, but was somewhat less pleased with the description in the (American) Rose-Growers' Annual:

'Eleanor Roosevelt – often disappointing in a bed but quite satisfactory up against a wall."

A smart man always knows what to say. A wise man knows whether or not to say it.

MAY

The following was heard outside Hagleys (now Hunter).

"Yer, Mildred, Ah wuz only thinkin' last night 'ow you dawn zee many people with raid 'air anymore laake you used to. It zeems to me, they'm all grey 'aired now."

"Well what about it?"

"Wull, idn't that what 'appned with the squirrels?"

"Ah'm blawd if you ind't right. Us ought to wraate ter Daivid Attenborough about it."

"I already 'eve but 'ee amb't answered."

—ooOoo—

I have been pondering just how enjoyable the *Henry Williamson* articles in the Woolacombe & Mortehoe News have been. What an evocative writer he was, even in his early years, and it is good to see his words being appreciated and made available a century later. Evermore pertinent considering his local connections.

How well he sets down tales of wreckers and smugglers, and the macabre legend of Cap'n 'Arry's ghost riding his headless horse along Woolacombe Sands. As an amateur wordsmith, I have admiration (and envy) for those who can use our beloved language with such splendour but, sadly, it just serves to highlight the huge gap between fine writers and we amateurs.

—ooOoo—

Devonians have long been fond of similes and the following I remember from my youth. Readers will be able to add to the list:

On temperature – *As cold as a vrog*

On capacity – *As full as a' egg*

22

On weariness – *As tired as a fowl*

On cleanliness (lack of) – *As bissley as a toad* (I never understood that one)

On decay – *As rotten as a pear*

On common sense (lack of) – *As maize as a brish (brush)* (or, sometimes, *handcart*)

On beauty (lack of) – *As ugly as a box o' vrogs*

On meekness – *As mild as milk*

—ooOoo—

Yet another report, doubtless paid for directly or indirectly by the taxpayer, tells us that a certain university has discovered how *those in the know* have been underestimating the amount of alcohol being drunk by the average citizen as, apparently, they had not taken into account the increase being consumed at weddings, family parties etc., and whilst on holiday.

Now forgive me, but I didn't think it required a degree to work out that little gem; so here's a suggestion from one of the populace whose total academic achievements amount to one O-Level (English Language, surprisingly):

If successive governments, of whatever colour, were to spend more time concentrating on improving the quality of life of the electorate, and less on instigating fatuous surveys, perhaps we would not need to drink so much.

Just a thought but, again, the likes of us don't have any inroads into government. You need a degree you see.

—ooOoo—

Visitors to Ilfracombe Tesco will see a large neon sign outside – the name *Tesco* emblazed in blue and red. They are then presented with a noticeboard with *Tesco* prominently displayed on the top, as it is everywhere else, and given *Tesco* headed notelets in order to write comments on *Tesco*. So why, oh why, do they then write *"I really like Tescos. . ."*

Presumably these are the same people who shop in Marks & Spencer**s** and Etam**s**, and play Trivial Pursuit**s.**

I cannot recall our local supermarket ever having an 's' to finish its name in any of its incarnations, and yet people still patronised Ford & Lock**s,** Gateway**s** and eventually Somerfield**s.**

And yet no-one seems to shop at Co-Op**s.** Why would this be?

Answers on a postcard please.

—ooOoo—

We desperately need a lighter note and so I conclude this chapter with a Westcountry Medical Dictionary which may help visitors and new residents to our area. *(This has been passed to me and I am unable to identify the author but will happily give a credit if he or she can be identified.)*

Bacteria	Back door to the cafeteria
Barium	What doctors do when patients die
Benign	What you be after you're eight
Caesarean Section	A district in Rome
Cauterize	Made eye contact with her
Dilate	To live long
Enema	Not a friend
Fester	Quicker than someone else
Fibula	A small lie
Labour Pain	Getting hurt at work
Medical Staff	A doctor's cane
Morbid	A higher offer

Nitrates	Cheaper than day rates
Node	I knew it
Outpatient	A person who has fainted
Post Operative	A letter carrier
Recovery Room	Place to do upholstery
Secretion	Hiding something
Seizure	Roman emperor
Tablet	A small table
Terminal Illness	Getting sick at the airport
Tumour	One plus one more

THOUGHTS FOR THE MONTH

The test of our progress is not whether we add more to the abundance of those who have much, it is whether we provide enough for those who have too little.

Since at the beginning and the end of our lives we are so dependent on others' kindness, how can it be that, in the middle, we neglect kindness towards others? (His Holiness The Dalai Lama).

JUNE

THE FLY ON THE WALL

Where have all the flies gone? Not in the ointment it would seem.

In the 1950s, no self-respecting kitchen would be complete without the flypaper hung in a prominent position, countless dead insects attached to its agglutinated surface.

Long before the invention of computer games, children could entertain themselves by swatting flies with a rolled-up newspaper or, for the middle classes, a tailor-made plastic 'fly-swatter' from Timothy White's (2 shillings & sixpence including purchase tax).

There was even an advertising poster campaign with the header *Flies Spread Disease*. (It was not uncommon to see graffiti underneath adding *'keep yours zipped up'.*)

We were spurred on by explicit Public Service broadcasts, and newspaper articles, outlining the abominable habits of the common housefly as he transferred germs from general rubbish (or worse) onto food by a nauseating process of sucking and vomiting the bacterium.

The little beast would interrupt sleep, reading, television or (virtually) any indoor activity with his aerobatics and accompanying buzzing.

Well, either we were far more successful with our swatting skills than we realised, or the ecology has changed, but the common housefly now rarely puts in an appearance. So do we enjoy a resultant decrease in food-type poisoning as a result? It would seem not.

We now have salmonella, staphylococcus, bacillus cereus, campylobacter, e-coli, listeria, to name a few pronounceable ones, with which to contend.

Was life not simpler when any illness afflicting the general bodily area between the lungs and the genitals was simply referred to, in hushed whispers, as 'a bug'?

Should we campaign for the conservation of *musca domestica* (a rather banal Latin name which can be embellished by adding that the little beast is a diptera of the Brachyera sub-order, whatever that might mean?).

Would he now fight on our behalf against the rival viruses of twenty-first century living?

Would the twenty-first century juvenile set aside his Game Boy for the pleasure of a half-hour fly safari? Could 'Celebrity Insect Swatting' be the next reality abomination to grace our television screens (doubtless hosted by *Ant* and Dec, or even Stephen *Fly*).

But this is to trivialise the demise of an unloved creature who was a fixture of our not-so-distant past.

—ooOoo—

This weekend I managed something for the first time in over fifty years.

If this has grabbed the attention of anyone still reading, the reality maybe something of an anti-climax - I refer to watching the Eurovision Song Contest.

Yes, the last time I endured this ordeal was in the 1950s when Pearl Carr and Teddy Johnson were singing a ditty about a little bird (I might have that last part wrong, but no matter). This year I tuned in primarily at the behest of Ken Bruce and I was much amused when he related his (presumably tongue-in-cheek) list of handy translations of the phrases most likely to be needed by the BBC staff in Azerbaijan or somewhere equally obscure. These commenced with:

'Can I have a cup of tea?'

'Where are the toilets?'

'Honestly, officer, I never laid a finger on her.' and

'Can I see the British Consul?'

Sadly, Ken Bruce was compering the event for radio and was not to be seen on television, but where was Katie Boyle? Surely no Eurovision is complete without this doyenne of the airways? *(Publishers' Note: I think she died about forty years ago!)*

For those who were privileged to miss this extravaganza, our British entry performed first, which is not, perhaps, to our advantage. Now there is no questioning the *quality* of the performance (if indeed that be the word) and I know that the organizers will not be remotely interested in the opinions of a failed scribe from Woolacombe, and neither should they be, but, from my perspective, it gradually became apparent that we were out of kilter with the rest of Europe (and incidentally what a large continent 'Europe' now seems to be!).

Whilst the others entertained with spectacular light shows, fountains, and vibrant and glamorous young people in erotic dancing routines, our entry relied upon a static and ageing minstrel clad in black silk shirt and trousers, complemented by a silver medallion, crooning a ballad. It seemed, well - sort of past its sell-by date, more of a 1950s offering and not quite what the voting public were seeking, which soon became embarrassingly obvious.

The voice was still strong, and the lyrics had great eloquence but, presuming that 80% of those voting would not understand English, this was probably wasted.

It seems to me that an authentic representation of national tradition is what is required for success. (If this is not possible, then attractive young ladies dancing suggestively in minimal clothing will also do the trick.)

If we really cannot match the glamour of our fellow contestants, why not try tradition? It certainly worked for Russia with the grannies. Six historic dresses, and not many more teeth, they all looked so authentic that you really believed they could be packed inside each other at the end of the night in true Russian doll style; and they were runners-up to a lithe and lovely Swedish singer (dancing suggestively in minimal clothing, as it happens).

Might I suggest that next year we try something that truly reflects the U.K. in the twenty-first century?

For a start, we could have one or more young people dressed in the traditional garb of hoodie and trainers, spitting occasionally in the manner that has become their trademark. They could sing a song in 'txt spk' obviously using the 'words' 'm8' and 'lol' repeatedly, and perhaps selling a few copies of the 'Big Issue' between verses.

Surely that would capture the flavour of modern Britain and put us back at the top of the world?

Move over Sir Michael Grade, your job is in jeopardy.

OLD WOOLACOMBE & MORTEHOE CHARACTERS 4

And, perhaps, the *greatest* of all. Who can forget Stan Hunt supervising his yard up at the Station, a hundredweight bag of coal under each arm, ready for transference down to the South Street site?

Vasey, his trusted sidekick, was completely deaf and most instructions were conveyed with a system of hand signals – it worked, until Mrs Farson installed a new coal cellar in the celebrated house at Putsborough.

Older readers will remember the Farson family, famous author (James) Negley, and writer and broadcaster son, Daniel. It is Negley's widow to whom I refer.

"Mr Hunt," said she, "come down into the coal cellar and I will show you what the new system is to be." Stan dutifully followed her down and advised Vasey to await further instructions but, you see, the man was keen if nothing else. Stan and Mrs F had no sooner arrived in the coal cellar for her to show exactly where the product was to be delivered when Vasey emptied the first hundredweight of anthracite through the hatch, covering her in coal dust from head to foot, which was a sight many of us would have longed to see.

He used to relate how his good wife was a barmaid when they met, which was a little unusual and rather upsetting to her family. *"You've brought shame and disgrace on us",* her father allegedly said at their wedding. *"Firstly you go and work in a boozer and now you've gone and married one."*

His response when asked about the health of Mrs H? *"Oh, disagreeable as ever, Stefon* (don't ask), *I remind her she's got me but it doesn't seem to cheer her up."*

I was working at the Bay Hotel when Stan had retired from the coal business to start Hunt's Dairy - where the Captain's Table now operates - and we used to obtain the ice cream cornets through Stan. He would be sat at the window, this huge man in his vest, dispensing ice creams and *verbal Valium* to the customers. Meanwhile I am at the back of the queue.

"Yes, Stefon?" he bellows, temporarily ignoring the ten or so visitors in front of me queuing for their ice creams. "Well, Mr Hunt, can you order us another box of cornets, and we have some from last year and we want to know if they are still useable?"

A big smile crosses his huge countenance and the eyes sparkle as he responds to all:

"Certainly they'll be alright. If there's any weevils in them, I shakes the weevils out like this," (vigorous arm movements as he addresses the first lady in the queue) "and, if there's any mouse droppings that I have missed, I says 'That's bits of chocolate, Madam, I should charge you extra for those'."

Standing outside the Boathouse Café one winter's day, a lady and gentleman pull up to ask directions.

"Excuse me but can you direct me to XYZ Caravan Site?"

"Leave this to me" says the big man, "XYZ Caravan Site. (Name changed for obvious reasons.) That's ****** ****** isn't it? Now tell me, what would a nice lady like you be doing with ****** ******?"

"Oh, well," came the rather flustered reply, "he's advertised in the 'Journal' that he's got some caravans for sale and we were just going to look...."

"Ha – you be very careful, My Dear. You'll find that he's sold you a caravan and, when you turn around, he's stolen your car!"

I don't think the couple ever received the directions but they drove off in a state of some bemusement.

Despite being such a huge man, he was a delightful ballroom dancer and the last dance of the evening would always be Stan Hunt with Mrs Edna Pocock, another large but delightfully dainty lady on her feet, to the great rapture of all.

THE A.A. HANDBOOK

I refer to a lovely old tome in my possession, namely *The Automobile Association Handbook,* this one for 1939 - 40, which must have been a turbulent time indeed.

Nonetheless, dear Woolacombe & Mortehoe are rightfully listed and we learn that we are 'two hundred & eight *and a quarter* miles from London'. The preciseness is interesting and leads me to wonder exactly from where the measurements are taken. In the back of my mind I recall being told that it is from the main Post Office, which, in our villages, would not be difficult to locate, but where exactly would that be in the capital? Perhaps a reader can let us know.

Returning to the book, we are told that Licensing hours are 11 – 2 and 5 - 10 weekdays, and early closing, as we know, is Wednesday. (Does anyone observe Early Closing Day anymore?) The post is collected at 8.00 a.m. and 8.30 p.m., which seems a very long day for somebody. (Jimmy Smith perhaps?)

Turning to the hotels, and leading the field, as you would imagine, is the Woolacombe Bay, with its telephone number *Woolacombe 7*! It has 78 bedrooms, all with H & C *running* water; and a single bedroom will cost the princely sum of 7/6 to 10/6 per night (around 37 – 54 pence in today's currency).

Those looking for cheaper accommodation have a choice of the Rathleigh (older readers will not be surprised to see this listed as *Station* Road); Atlantic, Headlands, Beach, Cliffside, Hartland and Crossways. Curiously, the latter four are listed as 'Sea Front', 'The Parade', 'Esplanade' and 'Parade Road' respectively, despite all being situated on the same Sea Front.

Oddly, there is no mention of the Watersmeet.

Visitors preferring to stay in Mortehoe have but two choices – the Mortehoe Hotel; or Hillside Cottage where a single room is 4/- - 7/6 (20p – 37p) per night – taking a bath will cost an extra 6d (2.5p), breakfast 2/6 (12.5p) and high tea 2/- (10p).

THOUGHTS ON THE FIRST MARINE CONSERVATION ZONE

An annual trip to Lundy on a friend's boat provided our best dolphin 'encounter' to date. A school of around ten or fifteen Common Dolphins joined us about two miles off Lundy and stayed for around twenty minutes. How they seem to enjoy 'surfing' the bow wave and swimming below the boat only to emerge mischievously on the other side, and it is from a small boat that one can really get close to these beautiful creatures.

When else do we really get the opportunity to make eye contact with a truly wild creature - other than Friday night in Ilfracombe High Street obviously - but I jest, and my thoughts inevitably turned to the proposals in the Bristol Channel and the environmental catastrophe that we have, mercifully, been spared.

Not only the dolphin, but the Harbour Porpoise, the (Atlantic) Grey Seal and all our migratory seabirds would have been subjected to the devastating noise and vibration of eleven years of pile-driving, together with chemicals, whose provenance we know not, being injected into our seabed. This before the actual monstrosity was created. Surely those who survived would not remain in our waters? This would have been the destruction of the fantastic Marine Conservation Zone that has been successfully established around Lundy; and all for the greed of the power companies eagerly sucking up the subsidies so readily provided by the hapless consumer and taxpayer.

It would be nice to say that common sense eventually prevailed but the truth, as we know, was that it was a purely financial decision.

THOUGHTS FOR THE MONTH

I prayed and asked God for a new mountain bike but my teacher explained to me that God doesn't work in that way. So I stole a mountain bike and prayed for forgiveness.

In a recent interview, General Norman Schwarzkopf was asked if he thought there was room for forgiveness toward the people who perpetrated the 9/11 terrorist attacks.

His answer was classic Schwarzkopf:

"I believe that forgiving them is God's function, our job is to arrange the meeting."

JULY

July vourteenth and Mrs Gripepimple is complainnin' 'bout the weather.

'Er said er've never seed ought laake it. 'Well', zaid I, 'in that caise you shude ev been yer last year – t'was much wuss than this.'

Anyway, I pointed out to 'er that t'ev been baiking 'ot ev'ry day till 'er arrahved and us needs zome rairn. But that didn't zeem to cheer 'er fer zome reason, zo I told 'er the gude news:

'Tis gwain be much better termorro,' I zaid.

'Really?' 'er zaid.

'Yes,' I zaid, 'the rairn's gwain be coming strairt down instead of blawin in yer faice.'

Wull, ken 'ee b'lieve it? Er still wadn't 'appy zo I left the best bit of news till last:

'Tis gwain be eighty- two degrees on Vriday,' I zaid and 'er was wull pleased by that zo I didn't ev the nerve ter tell 'er that t'was gwain be vorty-wun in the morning and vorty-wun agairn in th' afternoon.

GOLF

'The lowest recorded score on any 18-hole course with a par score of 70 or more is 55 (5 under bogey) by A.E. Smith, the Woolacombe professional, on his home course on 1 January, 1936. The course measured 4,248 yards. The detail was 4,2,3,4,2,4,3,4,3 = 29 out, and 2,3,3,3,3,2,5,4,1 = 26 in. The last 9 was also a record low.'

So runs the opening entry in the five-page 'Golf' section of the very first Guinness Book of Records in 1955, and this stood for several decades. (The record that is; sadly not the course, which was destroyed in the war.)

I have a copy of the book, mine c1965, which I keep for posterity but, and here is an interesting fact – many people may not know that his caddy on the momentous day was none other than Mr George Hagley from the wonderful drapers and outfitters in West Road.

ON DAYTIME TELEVISION

As one who was always taught that you should try everything in life once, with the obvious exceptions of incest and Morris Dancing, it would now be appropriate to add 'watching daytime T.V.' to the list, having strayed into a house where this unfortunate pastime is the norm.

So, for any daytime T.V. virgins, permit me to give a resumé:

Firstly, a humourless little man in an ill-fitting grey suit appears and advises us that he is Jeremy Kyle. (Some poor souls may arise earlier and be subjected to even more moronic voyeurism but, mercifully, so far the writer has been spared the horrors of pre 9.00 a.m. offerings.)

Said Mr Kyle then regales the expectant viewer with details of the day's, well, contestants? culprits? misfits? Who knows how best to describe the unfortunates whose intimate relationships will be laid bare in a narcissistic display of their troubled lives?

We are introduced to the first dysfunctional member of society together with his, or her, warring partner/mother/illegitimate child/former lover or whatever is the flavour of the day, whereupon the proceedings commence with the main protagonist screaming, shouting and swearing at the other party, to the obvious delight and, dare I say, encouragement of the audience.

Mr Kyle appears to dispense some form of 'verbal Valium', giving occasional concerned (scornful?) looks to camera. This either results in a resumption of hostilities, or a tearful 'reunion' between two of the parties, to the obvious wrath of any third party who might have been dragged into the fray.

If reason fails – which, given the nature of the participants and the *raison d'être* of the show, is more than likely, 'Security' in the shape of one or more burly bouncers is called, with great drama; to the obvious delight of the baying audience.

But righteous indignation is the order of the day, and the said Mr Kyle brings the show to a close with a moralistic summary of the proceedings.

At the end of this ordeal, our spirits rise a little, with the arrival of Eammon Holmes and his minxish wife, Ruth.

But, alas, relief is short-lived.

There follows a hotch-potch of discussion, on subjects such as the antics from 'I'm a Celebrity' or the latest 'reality' offering, to which Eammon, to his eternal credit, at least manages an occasional incredulous look to camera.

However, a personal drama is called for, as no daytime programme is complete without one. Miss/Mrs X unleashes her emotional trauma upon us, but what can be done to help her? The answer is clear:

Cue old blond woman with long face and dreary voice:

"Deirdre, what is your advice to........?"

Well, you get the picture.

Despite Eammon's obvious charm, and Ruth's waspish half-smile and slight jerk of the head every time something vaguely risqué is mentioned, we are soon ready for the next offering, and we now reach the climax (no pun intended) of the day, in a programme with the dubious title of 'Loose Women' .

Here we have four, (or is it five, it's a job to tell) out-of-work actresses or over-the hill singers, pontificating on the trivia of the day.

The one on the right delights in regaling us about her rampant love life, the one to her left, apparently, is suffering the exact opposite, whilst the ex-singer keeps reminding us that she is 'a Northern Lass' although the relevance of this is never explained.

It cannot get much worse, and yet it does.

We are never far from double entendres relating to 'size' or 'positions', or any other example of what used to be known as schoolboy humour but now apparently rates as 'entertainment'. The whole is accompanied by much guffawing and raucous encouragement from the audience.

As to what happens in the afternoons, I am afraid that my stamina never allowed me to reach that particular pinnacle and I must leave it to another reader to enlighten you. I've cancelled my T.V. licence and taken up knitting.

'Nurse, The screens!'

On the subject of the aforesaid 'Loose Women', for those unable to satisfy their needs with an hour's television, there are, unbelievably, magazines available seemingly devoted entirely to the antics of the participants.

Biographies follow auto-biographies, 'Kiss & tell' articles, repeat articles, denial stories and much, much more are churned out in a never-ending stream of vapidity.

There is no opinion too trivial, no event too banal to attract media attention if the subject has appeared a few times on television and is thus in some people's eyes 'a celebrity'.

Incredibly, one inmate of the programme has even managed the double financial delights of a 'warts & all' autobiography, doubtless in full consultation with the husband & family, only to follow it with a printed 'Open Letter of Apology' to said spouse for printing the sordid story in the first place.

The sound of mutual, gleeful hand-rubbing in anticipation of not one, but two, large publisher's cheques being delivered to the household is almost palpable.

However, I must finish this article now as the latest edition of Slag Bag magazine has an interesting article on Jordan's new accessories and I must rush to Shirley's to secure my copy before it sells out.

ON BEING 'LOCAL'

We must consider the question of being 'local' and why, dare I say, some *non-locals* consider it such a divisive issue.

I hear a new-arrival in the parish laughingly advising that she "knows you have to be here x number of years before being considered 'a local'" and I wonder why so much is made of what is, to my mind, a really simple matter.

For, surely, the term 'local' is an adjective, no more no less. Much as someone might be described as thin/fat, short/tall, old/young, they are either local or not, depending upon whether they grew up here. This has no significance other than for identification or, if we know them to be 'non-locals', we would not bore them with stories about people who used to live here and in whom they could not possibly be interested.

If I were to move to, say, Barnsley, would I expect to be called a Yorkshireman? That would be nonsensical – I was not brought up there, I don't speak with their accent – but that would not be a matter of any contention, just a simple fact. Similarly, the term 'local' is interchangeable with Woolacombe (bred) or just Devonian, it does not imply anything more significant, and is not meant to be in any way contentious.

THOUGHTS FOR THE MONTH

Hospitality is making your guests feel like they're at home, even if you wish they were AND a diplomat is a person who will tell you to 'Go to hell' in such a way that you will look forward to the journey.

There are almost 5000 gods being worshipped by humanity. But don't worry, only yours is right.

AUGUST

SO NOW WE KNOW IT'S TRUE………

It seems that, despite what the economists, statisticians, politicians and all other 'experts' tell us, our parents and grandparents always knew best, and their opinion remains true today…. IF THE SUN SHINES, THE VISITORS WILL COME.

And what a summer the 2014 one has indeed been. Thankfully, a brilliant fine spell, that kindly included the peak holiday weeks, has produced a bumper crop of visitors.

Over recent years it has been fashionable for pundits to direct their 'considerable knowledge' to the holiday industry. We are advised that the problems are all because of economic circumstances; cheap foreign holidays (I have been guilty of spouting that one); Wimbledon fortnight (happens every year doesn't it?); European/World Cup (one every other year?); is it not great to prove them wrong and to reinforce the one fact that has held true throughout the years – it's all down to the weather?

So congratulations to all who have benefitted from that radiant ball in the sky and thank you for keeping faith over all those disastrous years. We know how dispiriting it has been but be comforted by the one overriding fact – if the weather co-operates, Woolacombe & Mortehoe can still provide the very best of holidays, and there is nothing to suggest that this will not continue for another century.

I must now turn to the wonderful display to mark the seventieth anniversary of the American 'occupation' of the villages. Those of us growing up after the war were filled with stories of the American G.I.s, and to move amongst the U.S. Military vehicles and other memorabilia was an emotive experience, particularly when we thought of the men who lost their lives, both here and in the subsequent invasion, for the sake of our freedom.

So Well Done to all for this fascinating exhibition. It was memorable for those who were here during that period; evocative for those growing up afterwards, and instructive to the young for whom WW2 is something of which to learn in history lessons.

It would be appropriate to finish with the old WW2 joke about the Americans and Sandy Lane but I don't suppose that I will be allowed (*'NO, you certainly will not,'* - Publisher.) so it just remains for me to hope everyone enjoys their time in the less frenetic weeks ahead.

P.S. If there is anybody left who does not know the joke referred to above, it can normally be heard in the Chichester Arms on Friday nights.

LIDL BY LIDL
(OTHER SUPERMARKETS ARE AVAILABLE)

I have been persuaded of the merits of our latest supermarket and have taken up the call *'If you are middle, go Lidl'*. (I believe this refers to middle-class but this is of no consequence here.)

One thing that intrigues is the rapid, not to say manic, pace of the cashiers as items are scanned and virtually thrown towards the bagging area – and customers are advised that there is no time to bag items at the checkout. Oh no, all groceries must be slung, with equal haste, into the shopping trolley, to be subsequently packed at leisure using the shelf provided for that purpose.

ADMIRABLE. This cuts, or should cut, the time spent at the shop. Except that it doesn't, for the simple reason that they have not taken into account the typical North Devon shopper.

Is it not amusing to watch as the cashier, having created a new record in flinging the most groceries through the scanner in record time, shouts 'Thirty-five pounds forty pee' to the little old lady who has no concept of the 'Lidl bagging arrangements' and has still only loaded two or three items into her bag?

'Ow much m'dear?'

'Thirty-five pounds, forty pee.'

'There's no need to shout. I'll just vaand me purse.'

Handbag is then thoroughly searched until purse is located with some glee. *'How much?'*

'Thirty-five pounds, forty pee.'

'Yer you be – ten, twenty, thirty.' Notes are meticulously counted out. *'Oh, 'ebm quite got enough – I'll ef to give 'ee a card.'*

Notes are equally carefully replaced in purse, apart from the one that slips from the good lady's hands and is retrieved from under the desk by another customer. Purse replaced and handbag searched once again. Credit card eventually found. *'Where d' I put 'n een?'*

It is a case of 'old meets new', and my sympathies lie firmly with the old, so it is with some delight that I notice a complete change this week. The manic delivery is gone, to be replaced by a leisurely (but still efficient) bagging and payment process.

What has happened? Surely the mighty Lidl corporation cannot have succumbed to 'our' way of doing things? Could they have made an allowance for our more-leisurely, and greatly-coveted, pace of life?

Diary.

To Mortehoe for a pint or two in each of the hostelries. 'Difficult to imagine anything more agreeable, but then.....

On my return, the full horror of twenty-first century television. Two persons of limited stature - I hope I have phrased this in a politically correct manner - Ant & Dec. (Ant is the one who stands on the right, or is that Dec – no matter.)

Said persons are dressed in black tie and are presenting two 'celebrities' (I use inverted commas advisedly as I have not a clue as to their identities), but *celebrities* nonetheless are provided with a three-course meal contrived from the very genitalia and rectal passages of various insects, amphibians and smaller mammals (and here I kid you not).

Said celebrities then proceed to ingest the gastronomic imbroglio, the whole process captured by varied close camera angles lest the viewer should miss any of the finer points of the spectacle.

We are then treated to the reverse process as the ingestation is coughed, vomited or otherwise thrown up, all again portrayed by intimate camera angles, and the whole accompanied by a guttural and abdominal soundtrack, along with much clapping and cheering from aforementioned persons in black ties.

What am I describing? Is this a twenty-first century updating of one of Ken Russell's most revolting, yet so far unreleased, films? Is it, perhaps, a bad dream from which you will awaken, traumatised but grateful for your escape?

No, dear reader. This is PRIME TIME SATURDAY NIGHT TELEVISON VIEWING –'*I am a Celebrity –Get Me Out of Here'* is the name of the programme and, again, I use italics advisedly, as including the word 'celebrity' in the title takes considerable nerve in this writer's opinion.

According to aol who control my computer (for reason that I know not), 'Britain is gripped in its seasonal bout of jungle fever'.

Well, sadly, not this Briton, and not, I suspect, many millions more.

We have no need to go back to the early 1960s (but I will), just to remember the gentility of such offerings as Dixon of Dock Green – compulsory Saturday night viewing; Arthur Haines, Dave King, Bob Monkhouse, Benny Hill (before the word sexism had been invented), dramas, variety shows, quizzes. In turn, the 1980s, 90s and onward all provided captivating viewing. So how have we come to this?

American television was once described as 'One hundred channels and nothing worth watching'. The idea was incomprehensible to the British viewer with two, maybe three, channels of such high content that there was often conflict over which one to watch. (Fortunately disputes were later resolved with the advent of the video recorder.)

How have we reached this stage? Is this progress – to have achieved a level of mediocrity comparable to 1970s America? Answers on a postcard please.

Following evening

Mercifully a prior engagement spares me the ordeal of watching the finals of 'The X Factor', but, before I can make my escape, I am subjected to the opening where the compere rather optimistically welcomes viewers with the words 'Good Evening Britain' – a slightly exaggerated and pompous stance for a second-rate talent show, one would have thought.

I am afraid I have no idea of the subsequent results; if you are remotely interested you will no doubt have found out this information on the night. For my part I am just grateful that I can now turn on the computer without being subjected to the words of wisdom from Tullisa (or is it Towie?). One of the many benefits of (late) middle-age is that you are no longer required to have an opinion on such matters.

Fortunately, this diet of non-stop rubbish has done me no harm and, if you will excuse me, I must now tune in to an unmissable 'Loose Women' Special on breast implants.

'Nurse, He's out of bed again!'

THOUGHTS FOR THE MONTH

As this chapter has been of a rather sombre nature, I am reminded that there are only two letters different in the words 'sombre' and 'sombrero' but it becomes a vitally important distinction if contained in the dress code for a funeral.

Should you ever find yourself the victim of other people's bitterness, smallness or insecurities, remember it could be worse – You Could Be Them.

SEPTEMBER

"They zay 'Combe ev 'ad a fantastic zummer fer traide, Mildred."

"Wull, us want to get Daimian 'Irst down yer, like they've got – that's why they'm doing so well."

"Oh well, ee wuz a gude footballer – if twadn't fer ee's dree goals us wouldn't ev won that World Cup you naw."

"Naw maid, that's Geoff 'Irst – I'm telling about the faimous artist, Daimain 'Irst. He've got a shop in Ilfracombe. He maikes skulls with diamonds all over em', then ee puts daid sheep in preservative and people buys em to put in their lounges."

"What, be em maize?"

"Naw, Maivis, tis all the raige fer rich volks. But, you zee, while ees zeliin' they skulls fer vivty million pounds a tahme, us is down yer selling buckets & spaides fer a couple o' quid. 'Tis no gude fer bringing money into the parish. Zee, another thing. In Combe they've got a 'café zoziety."

"Wull, us got cafés down yer – plenty of em."

"Naw naw Mavis, that's naw gude –you need a zoziety. Rich people likes to drink their tay in a zoziety."

"Wull, us got to move with the tahmes ah spawse' What d' 'ee zay 'ee puts they sheep een?"

ON THE SCARECROW FESTIVAL

Standing enjoying a pint outside the Chichester Arms a few weekends ago and I am troubled by the number of young persons staring at me before writing something down on a piece of A4 paper. It is only when one child has the temerity to ask "Which character are you supposed to be?" that I realize that it is the Scarecrow Festival and I should really dress with a little more care and move about slightly.

But I jest. What a fun weekend that was and many congratulations to the participants who put in so much work and thought to creating those lifelike models. The whole event was enjoyed by young and old alike and was a credit to the village, so well done to one and all.

On a serious note, children, the Scarecrow Festival has now finished, I am sorry to disappoint you and, yes, I know, some of you did get excited at the sight of some ragged individuals, holding pints of beer, outside the Ship Aground on Friday night but, sadly, they were not scarecrows, although I agree they would have scared our avian friends and many others. It is perfectly understandable that you thought you recognised Wurzel Gummidge, the resemblance is uncanny but, unfortunately, it was a lookalike from Rockfield Road. Sorry to end on a disappointing note.

ON COMPENSATION

It is a long-held tradition in England that we help each other – things go wrong, mistakes are made, BUT we have always endeavoured to put it right. Sadly, this is no longer the case due to the omnipresent fear of....LITIGATION. 'Never admit you are wrong' is now the mantra, in case of the dreaded 'L' word. It's all about 'damage limitation' you see (another buzzword). But how did we come to this?

Mr or Mrs Average never dreamt of taking court action until all these opportunities of easy cash were forced upon them by aggressive TV advertising and constant unsolicited telephone calls.

We recently had the case of a lady burning her mouth on a hot pasty, which, incredibly, commanded several column inches in the 'N.D. Journal' and culminated in the depressingly predictable paragraph where we learn that m'learned friends have already been instructed and a large compensation cheque is eagerly awaited.

When will this madness cease?

It is interesting to note in this case that the good lady was 'disappointed' with Messrs Warrens' response when they apparently apologised and pointed out (not unreasonably) that 'hot pasties do come out of a hot oven'. This leads us to ask exactly what action she would deem appropriate?

Should the baker perhaps employ a Health & Safety Operative (having given due regard to gender, ethnicity and sexual orientation) to point out to customers that hot pasties can be, well, hot?

Perhaps ice cream vendors would need to advise customers that their wares can be cold; or would hoteliers with en-suite bedroom facilities be prudent to advise customers that showers can sometimes be wet?

As a North Devonian, I had always believed that our inherent pragmatism would spare us much of this insanity. Sadly, my optimism seems to have been misjudged.

But where will it end? And this time the question is not rhetorical. Does no-one consider the time and worry, to say nothing of the costs, that these actions can cause? Is it too late to suggest that common sense might once again raise its head in our judicial system?

We simply cannot go on, year in year out, favouring ever more ludicrous claims from people who, frankly, should not be allowed further than their front gate. The burden is now unsustainable.

I apologise (well, not too deeply actually) to the insurance industry and the legal profession but, clearly, the whole thing is financially imbalanced.

To take an example, it seems that the County Council cannot afford to repair the potholes and other damage to the roads because they are paying out so much in compensation to motorists/cyclist/pedestrians for damage or injuries sustained by potholes. Now, I am no economist but surely the obvious solution is staring us in the face?

It will take considerable litigation to reverse this obnoxious trend and, with politicians largely coming from a legal background, it will not be easy, but action has to be taken before many of us are either bankrupt or insane.

—ooOoo—

Sitting on the school bus the other morning and listening to the conversation in front of me, I realised that some things never change:

"I don't want to go to school, Mum, all the teachers hate me."
"Well you have to go to school and that's the end of the matter."
"But I don't want to – all the children are unkind to me."
"Well you have to go, Son, you're the headmaster."

On a serious note, I have never noted so many stories and pictures of children's first days at school until this year (unsurprisingly the Greetings Card manufacturers – never slow to recognise a bandwagon – are now firmly on board).

New pupils start with just half a day or, in one case, the parents choose the hours of attendance that the child would most appreciate. None of this is a bad idea but what a contrast to our young days:

Reminiscences abound of the 1950s and being dragged up to Woolacombe Primary School *kicking and screaming* – literally.

Between sobs: *"I don't want to go to school – Mr Rigby hits me and shouts at me. I'm frightened."* Sadly, all protestations fell on deaf ears of course. Much as some of our parents felt exactly the same emotions as those of today, ultimately it was a question of 'get in there and get on with it'.

On a lighter note, I am reminded of a poem for the occasion:

The first day at his new school – he's frightened and he's weak
He stands there in the playground too terrified to speak
He starts to cry, he wets himself, and then he has a thought:
This really shouldn't happen – to a man who teaches sport.

THOUGHTS FOR THE MONTH

The early bird might get the worm but the second mouse at the trap gets to eat the Cheddar.

Austerity – punishing the poor for the misdeeds and mistakes of the rich.

OCTOBER

THOUGHTS ON AUTUMN

It seems unbelievable that we are now in October, *'when the voice of nature is hushed and preparation is made for sleep, and a time of refreshment, before the herald of Spring'.*

As we contemplate the miracle of the ever-revolving seasons, we trust that those who have toiled so hard in our holiday trade can now also enjoy some well-earned rest and relaxation.

But now a moan.

The annoying trait of abbreviating virtually every word in our beautiful language continues unabated – young people now go to *'uni'* and eat *'sarnies'* – ugh. However, the problem now arrives on our shores with the irritating trend of newcomers to the parish calling our beloved village *'Wooly'.*

Please desist. I know we talk of 'Morte' but this is traditional - Morte Point, North Morte etc. But *'Wooly'* - really! It does grate on the ears. Let *Woolacombe* have its full name say I.

It is the strict teaching of grammar, punctuation and syntax that makes sense of the English language. Who remembers the old spelling rule: 'I' before 'e' except after 'c'? To which we would respond: 'But, a *weird* man *seized Sheila* by the *weir'.*

But there are even more important issues:

Our first English lesson. Ilfracombe Grammar School, September 1960 and the question posed was 'How important is punctuation?'

Answer 'Life or death'.

How is this possible? Consider the telegrams that were sent at the time where there was no provision for punctuation. You might have read:

"SHOOT THE SENTRY ON NO ACCOUNT SHOOT THE GUARD DOG."

Dependent on whether the punctuation mark was intended to be placed after 'sentry' or after 'account', the wrong one could easily lose their life. As we were taught, 'Life and death'.

Many will remember another common example of 1960s' grammar in the sentence:

"The boy said the teacher is an idiot."

You are probably way ahead of me here but who is defaming whom?

Do we mean:

The boy said, "The teacher is an idiot."

Or

"The boy," said the teacher, "is an idiot."

Now I notice a disturbing, although somewhat humorous misuse of the word 'literally'.

Surely, the whole intent of the word is to stress the factual nature of a statement, lest it were to be taken metaphorically. But, no, I have heard no less than three recent examples:

A Cabinet Minister, who should know better, (on reflection, perhaps not) when debating the very serious issue of care for the elderly, advised that 'It has been proven that, when older people go into homes, they *literally* go down-hill a lot more quickly.'

Now, I do not want to trivialise what is a very important issue but does he *literally* mean *literally*? Is someone greasing their backs, or fitting them with castors?

I am not intending to be offensive here but surely we should be able to rely on senior government ministers to use the correct phraseology when debating matters as serious as this?

I leave you with two more, both heard on the radio:

A young pop music promoter, when regaling us of the merits of his latest fledgling band, opined: "We knew that, when the first two records sold so well, the third would *literally* walk out of the shops on its own."

That would have been interesting to observe, but my favourite came during a recent football match. When the pundit was asked at half-time what he thought the losing manager would be saying to his team, he came out with this gem:

"Well, I think he'll be telling them to *literally* throw everything except the kitchen sink at (the opposition) in the second half."

How do you suppose the referee would handle that one?

Here endeth the first lesson, and I shall try to be a little less pompous in future.

—ooOoo—

I was reminded of an entry in my last book attacking a certain Mrs Mills (no, not that one) for her vitriolic attack on Woolacombe in the 'Sunday Times' and how she had launched an attack on of our most characterful houses, The Outlook. What should be done to it? Mrs Mills had the answer: *"Knock the whole first floor into one mighty sixty foot living space, and give it a full-length picture window"*, presumably complete with stainless steel accoutrements – yuk.

Well I am pleased to say that the new owner ignored Mrs Mills and tastefully extended and improved the property, which now looks extremely attractive and in keeping with our other lovely architecture, not least the neighbouring property 'Swiss Cottage' (formerly Kites' Hill), where the new owners have, again, eschewed the garish original plan and created another delightful house.

We appreciate the thought that has gone into these developments and, for once, applaud the Planning Authority for their good sense.

—ooOoo—

I finish with a story of two men, both severely ill, lying in a hospital ward.

Of course time dragged, but the highlight of the day occurred when the man lying next to the window would raise himself from the pillow and, to the rapture of the other, he would describe the vista outside the window.

No detail was too small to be overlooked and his graphic illustration of the scenes filled his listener with a great sense of joy and hope.

There was a beautiful park with a stream meandering through, and a lake where ducks and other waterfowl would swim, play and raise their young.

Children fed the ducks and delighted in other games. Young lovers strolled hand in hand, and older people would come just to sit on the benches and take in the view.

One day there was a parade and the man described in great detail the bandsmen in their smart uniforms and the excited crowds watching.

He was a gifted orator and the daily recital was an enormous comfort to his friend.

Tragically, one morning the man by the window did not awaken. He had passed away in his sleep and his companion mourned the loss more than he could have ever anticipated. In particular, he missed the daily picture that had been described so vividly and so, after a respectable time, he asked if he could be moved to the bed against the window.

His wish was granted and, on the first day, he excitedly levered himself up to see out, only to be horror-struck to find that it faced nothing more than a blank wall.

His first feeling was one of deception: he felt he had been misled by his friend. He felt cheated and he made his feelings known to the nurse, who patiently explained to him that the man had been totally blind and would have had absolutely no idea what could be seen from the window.

"Perhaps he just wanted to bring some joy into your life and lift your spirits," she opined.

Perhaps there is a lesson there for us all.

THOUGHTS FOR THE MONTH

To steal one person's work is called plagiarism. To steal many people's is called research.

If intelligence mattered in regards to who should and shouldn't be used for food then there'd be a whole lot of humans on dinner plates tonight. (Randy Sandberg).

NOVEMBER

I was asked what arrangements I had made for the *'trick or treat'* which was apparently to be inflicted upon us on 31st October and my answer was unequivocal:

'I keep a bucket of water behind the door in readiness.' That, I find, is the best discouragement for this ghastly American practice which is seeping into our lives. And whilst on the subject of American traditions, we now have Black Friday. **Black Friday** – have you ever heard such nonsense?

What is it? Ah, well, nobody knows for sure. A quick trawl of the internet advises that it is either so-named due to the heavy traffic that occurs the day after Thanksgiving; or it is the day when retailers hopefully go 'into the black' in their finances, having traded at a loss from the start of the year until now (unlikely I would have thought) or, it was the day when, historically, slaves were sold to make way for the new influx shortly to arrive – which is a truly appalling thought.

Now forgive me, but none of these would seem a remotely worthy cause to 'celebrate' even if we knew for sure what we were celebrating but, as we don't, what is the point? Our American friends may well be daft enough to recognise a day of which no-one is sure of the origins, but surely we don't have to follow?

Anyway, back to Hallowe'en and, in my young day, we just didn't *have it*. Nobody could have told you what date Hallowe'en fell on and, equally, nobody cared. Our night was *Guy Fawkes Night,* and we 'did' it with gusto.

Boys (and some girls) congregated expectantly in the bus shelter until the appointed time, and then hours of innocent fun were to be enjoyed as we careered around the parish *lighting up* everyone's lives in the most *literal* sense.

How Alfie Parkhouse must have enjoyed chasing us down South Street with the broom in his hand! And what of the time Ivy joined in the fun by throwing the contents of the chamber pot at the assembled rabble (sorry, I meant group of young innocents)?

Even Ella Mills put aside her sometimes-disagreeable persona on November 5th and joined in the fun by blocking up her letterbox with old rags thus ensuring that, when the expected firework was pushed through, it caused a blaze enabling Ella to enjoy her own personal bonfire there in her porch.

And how jolly Cyril Liverton and his firecrew must have chuckled as they joined in the fun extinguishing the blaze, safe in the knowledge that the annual tradition of a call-out following a 'penny banger and letterbox incident' was still being preserved.

Sadly, long gone are these days of innocent childhood fun, to be replaced by what? Young people banging on doors and demanding, with menaces, to be given a 'treat'. What sort of society have we become, I ask?

On the subject of traditions, what became of May Day and dancing around the Maypole? (In Ilfracombe, we didn't have a Maple so we danced around The Co-Op - readers under 50 please ask an older person to explain.)

OVERHEARD OUTSIDE LONDIS:

"Yer, Maivis, whas 'em doing up at the Narrercett?"

"Ebm 'ee yeard? They recken thy'm gwain open th' Cabaret Bar agen."

"Get on with 'ee."

"Naw. Tis true. They've got the Westcoast Cleaners back for the fust naght."

"I think you'm getting mixed up there M'Dear, West Coast Cleaners wuz Chris Rowe's cleaning company in Arlington Plaice. You'm thinking o' the West Coast Zound."

"Aye, them, and they zay Roy's been intervooing the groups agairn and The Swingin Blue Jeans is gwain be playin agairn next month."

"Well, 'ow old be they now?"

"Wull, must be nantey if they'm a day but no matter. Shall us git out our best frocks and go up there agairn?"

"Ma dear, I'm certainly up for't. I just gotta vand my walking frame so's I can get up they steps. I wonder if Chris Pugsley's still behand the bar?"

THE ATLANTIC ARRAY

So the monster is dead – or at least put to an interminable sleep. The environmental and economic catastrophe that loomed so large has been extinguished, hopefully forever. A victory for common sense, a victory for the environment, for marine mammals and all sea life; for the already hard-pressed electricity consumer and the even harder-pressed lower-income residents of our country and, above all, a huge relief for the people of this parish.

We have been saved the agony of twelve years of pile-driving, and the untold damage that this would have inflicted on our marine life, fishing and holiday industry.

Moving on, we have now been presented with an opportunity, a chance to examine the *truly* workable alternatives for green energy in a rational way. A chance for opposing factions to join together in pursuing new and exciting developments that can bring untold benefits to the planet without the environmental disadvantages of the Array.

And alternatives present themselves here in North Devon, as nowhere else in the world, with our tides and marine currents.

We are all 'environmentalists', so let us move forward together, free from the greed of big business, from the dictates of Brussels and the self-interest of some in Westminster and beyond.

ON THE STORMS OF 2014

Turning to the recent devastating weather, was it not truly amazing to see the amount of debris washed up and to contemplate the mammoth job of clearing it? That huge tree trunk by the Boat House for instance.

Amongst others picking though the flotsam, I met a man who had collected enough decking timber to install a new garden feature. I was reminded of dear old Sid Norman who used to push his barrow along the beach in the 1950s every day collecting driftwood for his fire. What a bonanza Sid would have enjoyed!

It was also interesting to see the old steps exposed at the main beach entrance again, and to note the pristine condition of the Marland and red brickwork, showing no deterioration after having been preserved in sand for so many years.

—ooOoo—

A report in the W & M News of the delightfully-named 'Knit and Natter' in Mortehoe reminded me of a neighbouring parish, where they would consider themselves a little 'posher' than ourselves. The local Ladies' Group there meet to do embroidery which is known colloquially by the *dowagers* of the village as *Stitch & Bitch*.

THOUGHTS FOR THE MONTH

In the sixties, people took Acid to make the world appear weird. Now the world is weird so people take Prozac to make it appear normal.

There are some people who are always angry and continuously look for conflict. Walk away; the battle they are fighting is not with you, it is with themselves.

DECEMBER

Well my ancient T.V. finally went *on the blink* and, as I had promised myself, I did not replace it. Thus it was my firm belief that I wouldn't need a T.V. licence.

Not so now apparently.

I have been asked to *prove* that I don't have one. Well, as we know, proving a negative is not so easy but I have invited the powers that be to come around and check for themselves.

Not to be outdone, they have asked if I have a computer. 'Because you may watch BBC television on your P.C.' Well I might, but I don't. In any case it is supposed to be a TV licence, not a computer licence and, like everyone, I pay for the privilege of broadband anyway.

But you can't fight for ever and, having paid out £135, my thought is that I might as well pay another £200 and buy a TV.

Not so simple. No longer is it possible to switch on the Murphy or Baird and wait five minutes for the tube to warm up. One look at the Which TV page and I am filled with dread:

Freeview/Preview/Sea view? H.D./H.P? Plasma? - Plasma, that's blood isn't it? (Evidently not.) 3D/LED/LCD/DVD/BBC/HTV/PVC? HD-ready or not? Flatscreen/Fatscreen. 'Smart T.V. (as opposed to...?) What can it all mean?

So I am sorry to say that, if you think your humble scribe will be filling his time with the *meaningful* pastime of watching 'Under the Hammer' and those ghastly women on every lunchtime, as opposed to inflicting the dear readers of the local books and magazines with the regular nonsense, then I'm afraid the time is not yet ripe.

THOUGHTS ON CHRISTMAS

On a serious note, as I write this, Christmas is upon us, although it hardly seems so, and I put this down entirely to the multi-national retailers, advertising buffs and others who, for their own avaricious motives, try to lengthen the pre-Christmas build up. **IT CANNOT BE DONE.** There are 'Twelve Days of Christmas' and, as far as I know, not one of them occurs in November (or before). Any thoughts of extending Christmas to what is really the end of the Summer merely dilutes the whole experience.

I visited Ashford Garden Centre, and please note this date as it is significant, on *OCTOBER 23rd*, and the Christmas display was in full swing. At the checkout, and here I kid you not, I was serenaded by Chris Rea's *'Driving home for Christmas'.*

Now, either he has a particularly good job if he can 'drive home for Christmas' on 23rd October, or something is seriously amiss, and I suspect the latter.

Let us keep all thoughts of Christmas until well into December when there may actually be some magic, and then the true 'Spirit of Christmas' might just reappear.

Also, let us not forget the Winter Solstice which is, or should be, a magical event, yet it is often a forgotten celebration.

Also known as 'Yule', the Solstice is generally celebrated on the 21st December (although the astronomical date changes from year to year – this year the actual Solstice takes place on the 22nd, at 00.22 a.m.). The Winter Solstice is the shortest day, and longest night of the year, and is the traditional time to celebrate the truly important things in life: family, children, home, and looking forward to a wonderful year to come.

Yule is a time that honours love and new birth, as well as the collective unity of man, and is primarily the celebration of the rebirth of the Sun. Many people associate the Winter Solstice, or winter itself, with death as it is the season in which nature is dormant, and in which many plants die off and crops are scarce. Conversely, the Winter Solstice is also the turning point of the year as, following this night, the sun grows stronger in the sky, and the days become gradually longer once more. Thus the Winter Solstice is also a celebration of rebirth from which we can all take comfort, and look forward with renewed hope.

When we add this to the very *raison d'être* - the Nativity, this is a truly magical time of year so it is dispiriting indeed to see and feel it characterised by the frenzy of shoppers, their faces a picture of worry over the Christmas dinner, their minds weighed down with last-minute gift apprehensions. I wonder how we have come to all of this?

With very best wishes from your curmudgeonly scribe anyway.

THOUGHTS ON BOXING DAY

I have expressed this sentiment on more than one occasion but, at the risk of offending anyone, *(Publishers' Note: it would appear that's never stopped you before.)* I, for one, am glad that it is over.

What was once a celebration of the birth of God's son, or just a joyous occasion, depending on your personal views, seems to have turned into an orgy of consumerism and greed on a totally inappropriate scale.

What we have lost, it seems to me, is that most precious thing – *simplicity*. Of course, the magic of Christmas for the children is of paramount importance, but a little more concentration on the enchantment of the event, rather than what *smartphone* they might be getting would not go amiss.

Truly, the decorations, the tree, visits to Santa etc. are to be cherished, but is it not possible to enjoy these with a little more enthrallment and, more importantly, a little less hysteria? And, I must ask, has it resulted in any more happiness? Do the participants of this frenzy, the vast majority being the ladies who have this work and worry foisted upon them, actually derive enjoyment any longer?

To read of the amount the 'average' family now spends on Christmas - many of whom surely cannot afford this extravaganza without the assistance of the credit card, or worse - is surely cause to weep. And this is to say nothing of the obscene amounts of food being purchased, much of it totally wasted, in this gargantuan feast of gluttony.

It is not for me to add to the long list of *'Have we lost the meaning of Christmas?'* articles, but I think the answer is apparent in the very dialogue every year:

The ubiquitous, *'All ready for Christmas?'* before the event, suggesting it to be some Herculean task that we all have to face with fortitude.

The *'Thank you for your card'* which elicits the response *'Oh. Thank you for yours'*, followed by mutual sniggering as if it is somehow the most humorous and witty exchange and, finally, the ever-present question afterwards: *'Had a good Christmas?'* to which the reply is always, ALWAYS, the same: *'Yes,* (pause) *quiet'*.

As opposed to what exactly, and why do we have this farcical and tedious interchange? '

Is it now too late to return to the magical, less materialistic celebration?

Don't ask me - I only pose the questions, but I am sure I am not alone in this wish.

THOUGHTS FOR THE MONTH

Why do they sterilise the needle for lethal injections?

We are buried beneath the weight of information, which is being confused with knowledge; quantity, which is being confused with abundance, and wealth, which is being confused with happiness.

We are monkeys with money and guns. (Tom Waits).

PROLOGUE

'Having flung aside the sword, there is nothing except the cup of love which I can offer to those who oppose me. It is by offering that cup that I expect to draw them close to me. I cannot think of permanent enmity between man and man, and, believing as I do in the theory of rebirth, I live in the hope that, if not in this birth, in some other birth I shall be able to hug all humanity in a friendly embrace.'

A quote from Mohandas K. Gandhi, if you will forgive me finishing on a spiritual and, hopefully, optimistic note.

And what of the forecasts for this monumental time in our history?

Firstly, Professor Brian Cox advises that the Mayans did *not* predict that the world would end now. The scholastic interpretation, apparently, is that they foresaw the end of one epoch and the beginning anew and, indeed, this would coincide with the astrological charts as the world moves into the new 'great month' of Aquarius that will take us through the next two millennia. (Let us talk here of astrology in its real sense rather than the nonsense published in the newspapers daily.)

There is much to suggest a new order, and many people are feeling a sense of challenge, if not actual anticipation. Certainly, major changes are needed. We contemplate the plight of the starving millions, which is still not improving, and we contrast this with our 'land of plenty'. We see the remuneration of the bankers and other corporate excesses and we can contemplate greed in its full abhorrence. How many of us can confidently preach the benefits of capitalism now?

Again, a quotation, I am afraid. This time an old American Indian prayer:

'Look at our brokenness. We know that in all creation only the human family has strayed from the sacred way. We know that we are the ones who are divided, and we are the ones who must come back together to walk in the sacred way. Grandfather, Sacred One, teach us love, compassion and honour, that we may heal the earth and heal each other'.

Beautiful.

Many of us write for a hobby or, perhaps, to earn 'a crust'. We sit in front of a screen thinking, writing, altering, referring to the Thesaurus, re-writing and finally polishing, and still we cannot come close to matching the power of these simple words and beautiful use of the English language.

On this topic, let Silver Birch have the last word:

'Gradually the light of spiritual truths will break through. As our teaching grows in your world it will mean the end of all separateness between peoples. It will mean the end of

national barriers. It will mean the end of race distinctions, class distinctions, colour distinctions and all the distinctions between churches and chapels, temples, mosques and synagogues for, gradually, all will learn that they have a part of the Great Spirit's truth and that the part enshrined in the heart of every other religion in no way contradicts that part that is precious to them. So, out of the apparent confusion, the divine pattern will take its shape, and harmony and peace will come.

The new world will be filled with happiness and wisdom. Its foundation will be sure and strong.

One day, there will arise a new race who will recognise that all politics, religion, science and knowledge are part of one thing. Then pain, sorrow, fear, mourning and unhappiness will be banished and your world will be a place of smiles and happy laughter.

When people develop their gifts, which come from the Great Spirit, and use them for the benefit of others, then there will be built a system founded on that which is eternal.

Let us hope that this comes to pass, if not in our lifetime then perhaps in our children's.

FURTHER READING

Firstly, I am reminded of John Phillips' excellent collection of reminiscences entitled **'Around Woolacombe in My Days'**

Written in John's own relaxed style, he chronicles life from the 1930s onwards including the Second World War and the dramatic effects on Woolacombe and, indeed, its contribution to the war effort.

The reader is 'there' as he tells us of schooldays in the war years, Cowler's Garage, fishing in the bay, Barton Farm and a myriad other anecdotes.

We also have Mrs Bidgood's excellent book **'Two Villages'** which I understand is still selling in reasonable numbers and I am delighted to report that Miss Alice Trebble's lovely book **'A Woolacombe Childhood'** is back in print and widely available in the parish.

Miss Trebble's delightful narrative echoes a Woolacombe of a bygone era and is a 'must read' for anyone who lives in, or has a fondness for the parish.

Many congratulations to Sue Hill for her hard work in resurrecting this lovely book. Let us not lose this chance to retain these valuable archives for posterity, as they will undoubtedly be of great interest to our descendants in future years and, as the sales people say: 'When they're gone, they're gone'.

In addition, Sue's captivating book **'Woolacombe and Mortehoe in Old Postcards'** contains the most delightful scenes of our two villages, accompanied by an excellent narrative, and there is also **Woolacombe at War and Other Tales of Old Woolacombe** wryly written by 'Benn Gunn'. (I think it is an open secret that this was *our own* Gerald Fisher.)

For further information, please visit, or contact, Mortehoe Museum, 01271 870028, or email: susancon.hill@btinternet.com

It is also most interesting to see the wealth of memorabilia appearing on the Old Woolacombe & Mortehoe website and the subsequent comments from former residents.

Finally, I dedicate this book to all who have lived in, contributed to, or just enjoyed our lovely parish.

Steve Brown